New Netherland Settlers: The Barheit Family Revealed

A Genealogy of Hans Coenradt and Barentje Jans Straetsman, the Immigrant Ancestors of the Barheit Family of Albany New York

By Lorine McGinnis Schulze

ISBN: **978-1-987938-06-7**

Copyright © 2016
All rights reserved
Publisher Olive Tree Genealogy

Cover Image: Seal of New Netherland

The Seal of New Netherland created in 1623 displays a beaver with the legend SIGILLVM NOVI BELGII (The Seal of New Netherland). The crown at the summit represents the colony's royal Dutch source, while the rampant beaever on the empty field indicates the colony's activity of fur trading. The surrounding necklace of shells is wampum, symbol of the colony's wealth.

DEDICATION

This book is dedicated to my father Cecil Norman McGinnis.

Without the past we cannot build a future.

Table of Contents

Part I: The Dutch in New Netherland

Origins of New Netherland

On September 19, 1609, the East India Company ship Halve Maen (Half Moon), commanded by Henry Hudson, an Englishman working for Dutch businessmen who were seeking a passage to the Orient, reached the present-day Albany area. He had started up the Hudson River just 8 days earlier, on September 11. As the Half Moon lay at anchor, Hudson could see an island lying between two rivers to his north. To the west was a vast, unexplored wooded land.

In 1613, four years after Henry Hudson explored the river that now bears his name, a Dutch ship called the Tiger left Holland en route for the same waters. Adriaen Block, the captain, was an enterprising Dutchman who had made two earlier visits to these waters. The market for furs in Europe was growing, and Block's earlier visits had convinced him that he could fill his ship with furs which he could sell in the Netherlands as coats and hats.

Two months after he left the Netherlands, Block passed through the narrows that guard the entrance to what is now New York Harbour. Within a few weeks he was anchored at the southern tip of modern-day Manhattan Island, his ship filled with beaver and otter pelts. Unfortunately for Block and his men, the Tiger caught fire and burned. Block and his crew were stranded thousands of miles from home. Over the long difficult winter, Block and his men built a new ship, a 44 foot sailing vessel they named the Restless.

Cutting down trees and using whatever tools they could salvage from the Tiger, the men completed the ship by the spring of 1614 and prepared to sail home. It was on this return voyage that Block and his men discovered Long Island Sound. Block sailed into a freshwater river he named Fresh River (present day Connecticut River) and then dropped anchor at a place he called Hoeck van de Visschers or Point of the Fishers (present day Montauk Point). Having sailed completely around the long island, he claimed it for the Netherlands.

On reaching the Netherlands, Block appeared before government officials. After hearing his story they named the area he had surveyed (from Chesapeake Bay to Cape Cod) Nieuw Nederlandt (New Netherland). The name Nieuw Nederlandt appeared for the first time on October 11, 1614 in a resolution of the States General of the United Provinces. A charter concerning trading licenses between New France and Virginia was issued to merchants to begin trading, and a settlement was planned for the island where Block had built the Restless.

The goal of this newly formed New Netherland Company was to sponsor voyages to the area between 40 and 45 degrees north latitude -- the middle of present-day New Jersey to the coast of Maine. This huge region now had a formal, European name.

It wasn't long before the Dutch started construction on a log fort on an island at the northernmost part of the Hudson River that was navigable for their ships. This was near present-day Albany. At about the same time, merchants in the Netherlands formed a second business entity for the purposes of exploiting their new fur-rich land. This was the Charter of the Dutch West India Company (commonly referred to as the WIC) which was chartered by the States General on 3 June 1621.

The West India Company was designed to stand strong against Spain's interests in the New World. It was empowered to create colonies, settle people, attack Spanish vessels, conduct trade and make treaties with the Indians. The Province of New Netherland fell under the broad monopoly of this company. The capital of New Netherland was to be established on Manhattan Island and called New Amsterdam.

After the 3 June, 1621 Charter of the West India Company, Fort Orange was built. It was built as a redoubt, surrounded by a moat 18 feet wide, mounted with 2 heavy and 11 light cannon, and garrisoned by 10 to 12 men. Around this was clustered a tiny hamlet occupied by the factors and servants of the WIC, who claimed all rights to the entire Indian trade. Although the charter, stated in part that they were to "....advance the peopling of those fruitful and unsettled parts", colonization was not encouraged.

The first interest of the Dutch in the Netherlands was the fur trade. Thus the New World represented a business opportunity. By 1624 Dutch traders were establishing the fort near Albany. English colonists were in Virginia and Plymouth, and England was claiming the northeastern Atlantic Coast. Both the English and the Dutch laid claim to Long Island, where the Dutch took hold of the western end, and later, the English settled on the eastern end.

To bolster their own land claims, the Dutch began to establish more settlements. They sent groups of Walloons (French-speaking refugees from Belgium) to New Netherland. The first group of Walloons arrived on Niew Nederlandt in 1624 when approximately 30 families arrived. By 1626, these groups had a stronghold on Manhattan Island.

Peter Minuit arrived in New Netherland aboard the See Meeuw on May 4, 1626 to become Director of the Colony. He purchased Manhattan from the local Indians for 60 guilders' worth of trade goods. He ordered that the settlement should be located on the southern portion of Manhattan Island.

The Schaghen letter is the earliest reference to this this purchase. Peter Schaghen, the author, was the representative of the States General in the Assembly of the Nineteen of the West India Company. In the late summer of 1626 he reported the arrival of the ship Wapen van Amsterdam (Arms of Amsterdam) from New Netherland. In his report to the directors of the West India Company he announced the purchase of Manhattan Island for the value of 60 guilders. The original of this document is held by the Rijksarchief in The Hague. A copy of the document along with the English translation follows:

Rcvd. 7 November 1626

High and Mighty Lords,
Yesterday the ship the Arms of Amsterdam arrived here. It sailed from New Netherland out of the River Mauritius on the 23d of September. They report that our people are in good spirit and live in peace. The women also have borne some children there. They have purchased the Island Manhattes from the Indians for the value of 60 guilders. It is 11,000 morgens in size [about 22,000 acres]. They had all their grain sowed by the middle of May, and reaped by the middle of August They sent samples of these summer grains: wheat, rye, barley, oats, buckwheat, canary seed, beans and flax. The cargo of the aforesaid ship is:
7246 Beaver skins
178½ Otter skins
675 Otter skins
48 Mink skins
36 Lynx skins
33 Minks
34 Weasel skins

Many oak timbers and nut wood. Herewith, High and Mighty Lords, be commended to the mercy of the Almighty,

Your High and Mightinesses' obedient, P.Schaghen

Image Courtesy of New Netherland Project, New York State Library

Soon a tiny community was built on the southern tip of Manhattan Island and called New Amsterdam by the Dutch. It was walled off to the north by a thick forest laced with Indian trails. Trees were cut down and small houses were erected. Dirt cart paths became streets. Windmills for making flour were built at the tops of creeks; sailing vessels lined new docksides. To the east, across what is today's East River, lay Long Island.

There was too much to be gained financially by not allowing further colonization. Eventually the Directors in Amsterdam were forced to find a remedy. On the 7th of June 1629, under the title of Freedoms and Exemptions, Patroons, those individuals authorized to establish plantations in Dutch New Netherland, were given freedom to bring colonists to New Netherland. Anyone who shipped 50 colonists to the New World at his own expense could buy land along the Hudson River. This man, called a Patroon, had complete jurisdiction and full trade privileges (excluding furs) in perpetuity for himself and his heirs. Thus a type of feudal system was begun in the New World.

The Directors in Holland rushed to avail themselves of the privileges; for the Charter offered them profit and gratification. WIC officials mainly wanted to make a fast profit and return home. They had the monopoly on the fur trade; so the Patroons had a slower rate of return from their initial investment, as well as losses from shipwrecks and Indian raids. By 1635 four of the five original Patroonships had failed, with the only remaining (and successful) one being Rensselaerswyck, run by Kiliaen van Rensselaer from the Netherlands.

The failure of the West India Company and the Patroons to fulfill the requirements of their charter with respect to colonization and encouragement of agriculture was so great that in 1638 the States-General was called on. The Directors were forced to proclaim free trade (including the all-important fur trade) and free lands to private persons under certain restrictions. This had the happy effect of stimulating immigration to New Netherland from the Netherlands. Willem Kieft arrived on board De Haring on March 28, 1638 to assume the directorship of New Netherland. One year later an enumeration of buildings erected for the West India Company on the Island of Manhattan, at Pavonia, The Bay, and Forts Orange, Nassau and Hope was completed.

Kieft's tenure from 1638 to 1647 was ruinous. As an administrator he was incompetent, and he did not accept any opposition.

By 1643 Kieft, in his lust for more land, had managed single-handedly to start a large-scale war, named the Kieft War. In 1643 war broke out across Manhattan and western Long Island that resulted in more than 1,000 Indian deaths, including a massacre in what is today Massapequa. Although several of Kieft's Officers objected to the plan to attack the starving and destitute refugees who had fled from their Mohawk enemies, Kieft insisted and on 23 February 1643 his men attacked with the resulting massacre leaving over 100 Indians dead. The results on the inhabitants of New Netherland was devastating as the remaining Indians quickly retaliated. Willem Kieft, recalled in disgrace to the Netherlands, was lost at sea on board the ill-fated Princess on his return trip in 1647. The Princess, carrying approximately 100 passengers, including Kieft, his next in command Cornelis Melyn, one of Kieft's most vocal opponents Domine Everardus Bogardus, and others, floundered off the coast of Wales and sank. Fewer than 20 men were saved; the rest, including Kieft and Bogardus, perished.

Of the earliest settlers, more than half were French speaking Walloons from what is now Belgium. Father Joque, a Jesuit missionary from New France (present day Quebec province) who was visiting the village in 1644 noted only ten thatched cottages. He also reported that there were four hundred people in New Amsterdam and 18 different languages.

Father Jogue wrote to his supervisors in France:

New Netherlands in 1644

By Rev. Isaac Jogues, S.J.

New Holland which the Dutch call in Latin Novum Belgium, in their own language Nieuw Nederland, that is to say, New Low Countries, is situated between Virginia and New England. The mouth of the river called by some Nassau river or the great North river (to distinguish it from another which they call the South river) and which in some maps that I have recently seen is also called, I think, River Maurice, is at 40°30'. Its channel is deep, for the largest ships that ascend to Manhattes Island, which is seven leagues in circuit, and on which there is a fort to serve as the commencement of a town to be built there and to be called New Amsterdam.

This fort which is at the point of the island about five or six leagues from the mouth, is called Fort Amsterdam; it has four regular bastions mounted with several pieces or artillery. All these bastions and the curtains were in 1643 but ramparts of earth, most of which had crumbled away, so that the fort could be entered on all sides. There were no ditches. There were sixty soldiers to garrison the said fort and another which they had built still further up against the incursions of the savages their enemies. They were beginning to face the gates and bastions with stone. Within this fort stood a pretty large church built of stone; the house of the Governor, whom they called Director General, quite neatly built of brick, the storehouses and barracks.

On this island of Manhate and in its environs there may well be four or five hundred men of different sects and nations; the Director General told me that there were persons there of eighteen different languages; they are scattered here and there on the river, above and below as the beauty and convenience of the spot invited each to settle, some mechanics however who ply their trades are ranged under the fort; all the others were exposed to the incursions of the natives, who in the year 1643, while I was there actually killed some two score Hollanders and burnt many houses and barns full of wheat.

The river, which is very straight and runs due north and south, is at least a league broad before the fort. Ships lie at anchor in a bay which forms the other side of the island and can be defended from the fort.

Shortly before I arrived there three large vessels of 300 tons each had come to load wheat; two had found cargoes, the third could not be loaded because the savages had burnt a part of their grain. These ships came from the West Indies where the West India Company usually keeps up seventeen ships of war.

No religion is publicly exercised but the Calvinist, and orders are to admit none but Calvinists, but this is not observed, for there are, besides Calvinists, in the Colony Catholics, English Puritans, Lutherans, Anabaptists, here called Muistes &c.

When any one comes to settle in the country, they lend him horses, cows &c, they give him provisions, all which he repays as soon as he is at ease, and as to the land he pays in to the West India Company after ten years the tenth of the produce which he reaps.

This country is bounded on the New England side by a river they call the Fresche river, which serves as a boundary between them and the English. The English however come very near to them, preferring to hold lands under the Dutch who ask nothing from them rather than to be dependant on English Lords who exact rents and would fain be absolute. On the other side southward towards Virginia, its limits are the river which they call the South river on which there is also a Dutch settlement, but the Swedes have at its mouth another extremely well provided with men and cannon. It is believed that these Swedes are maintained by some merchants of Amsterdam, who are not satisfied that the West India Company should alone enjoy all the commerce of these parts. It is near this river that a gold mine is reported to have been found.

See in the work of the Sieur de Laet of Antwerp the table and article on New Belgium as he sometimes calls it or the map; Nova Anglia, Novu Belgium et Virginia.

It is about fifty years since the Hollanders came to these parts. The fort was begun in the year 1615: they began to settle about twenty years ago and there is already some little commerce with Virginia and New England.

The first comers found lands fit for use, formerly cleared by the savages who previously had fields here. Those who came later have cleared in the woods, which are mostly of oak. The soil is good. Deer hunting is abundant in the fall. There are some houses built of stone; they make lime of oyster shells, great heaps of which are found here made formerly by the savages, who subsisted in part by this fishery.

The climate is very mild. Lying at 40 2/3 degrees; there are many European fruits, as apples, pears, cherries. I reached there in October, and found even then a considerable quantity of peaches.

Ascending the river to the 43d degree you find the second Dutch settlement, which the flux and reflux reaches but does not pass. Ships of a hundred and a hundred and twenty tons can ascend to it. There are two things in this settlement, which is called Renselaerswick, as if to say the colony of Renselaer, who is a rich Amsterdam merchant: 1st a wretched little fort called Ft Orange, built of logs with four or five pieces of cannon of Breteuil and as many swivels. This has been reserved and is maintained by the West Indis Company. This fort was formerly on an island in the river, it is now on the main land towards the Hiroquois, a little above the said island. 2ndly, a colonie sent here by this Renselaer, who is the Patroon. This colonie is composed of about a hundred persons, who resident in some 25 or 30 houses, built along the river, as each one found it most convenient. In the principal house resides the Patroon's agent, the minister has his apart, in which service is performed. There is also a kind of bailiff here whom they call Seneschal, who administers justice. All their houses are merely of boards and thatched. As yet there is no mason work, except in the chimneys. The forests furnishing many large pines, they make boards by means of their mills which they have for the purpose.

They found some pieces of ground all ready, which the savages had formerly prepared and in which they sow wheat and oats for beer and for their horses, of which they have a great stock. There is little land fit for tillage, being crowded by hills which are bad soil. This obliges them to be separated the one from the other, and they occupy already two or three leagues of country.

Trade is free to all, this gives the Indians all things cheap, each of the Hollanders outbidding his neighbor and being satisfied provided he can gain some little profit.

This settlement is not more than twenty leagues from the Agniehronons, who can be reached either by land or by water, as the river on which the Iroquois lie falls into that which passes by the Dutch; but there are many shallow rapids and a fall of a short half league where the canoe has to be carried.

There are many nations between the two Dutch settlements, which are about thirty German leagues apart, that is about 50 or 60 French leagues. The Loups, whom the Iroquois call Agotzogenens, are the nearest to Renselaerwick and Ft Orange. War breaking out some years ago between the Iroquois and the Loups, the Dutch joined the latter against the former, but four having been taken and burnt they made peace. Some nations near the sea having murdered some Hollanders of the most distant settlement, the Hollanders killed 150 Indians, men, women and children; the latter having killed at divers intervals 40 Dutchmen, burnt several houses and committed ravages, estimated at the time that I was there at 200,000 liv. (two hundred thousand livres) troops were raised in New England, and in the beginning of winter the grass being low and some snow on the ground they pursued them with six hundred men, keeping two hundred always on the move and constantly relieving each other, so that the Indians, pent up in a large island and finding it impossible to escape, on account of the women and children, were cut to pieces to the number of sixteen hundred, women and children included. This obliged the rest of the Indians to make peace, which still continues. This occurred in 1643 and 1644.

Three Rivers in New France,
August 3d, 1646.

On May 11, 1647 Petrus Stuyvesant arrived at Manhattan with the West India Company ships Groote Gerrit and Princess Amalia to assume his position as Director General of New Netherland. This position included the colonies at Curaçao, Bonaire and Aruba. At the start of Stuyvesant's administration, the population of New Netherland was an estimated 1,000 to 8,000. There is no exact count of the population at that time and only rough estimates can be made. By 1664 it was 10,000.

When he first arrived, Stuyvesant realized that English settlers were spilling into Dutch areas, so in 1650 he negotiated a treaty in Hartford. This treaty drew a line that began near present-day Greenwich, Connecticut, and crossed Long Island, beginning just west of what is now Oyster Bay. West of this line was Dutch, east of it was English.

In the early 1650s, the Dutch and English began fighting in Europe over trade and naval supremacy. This tension spilled over to the New World, where by the mid-

1660s the English were trying to oust the Dutch from New Netherland. Locally, there was a desire for more territory and the English were encroaching the Dutch borders.

In 1656 the WIC decided that "all mechanics and farmers who can prove their ability to earn a living here [New Netherland] shall receive free passage for themselves, their wives, and children" Colonists were granted as much land as they could cultivate, but without the privileges Patroons had formerly held. The result was an increase in population from an estimated 2,000 in 1648 to 10,000 in 1660. New Netherland changed during this time from a trading post to a colony.

List of Governors or Director-Generals of New Netherland

1624-1625 Cornelis Jacobsen May
1625-1626 Willem Verhulst
1626-1632 Peter Minuit
1632-1633 Sebastian Jansen Krol
1633-1638 Wouter Van Twiller
1638-1647 Willem Kieft
1647-1664 Peter Stuyvesant

Rensselaerswyck Beginnings

Rensselaerswyck was the name given to the large tract of land granted to the wealthy Dutchman and Patroon, Killiaen Van Rensselaer in 1632. It included all the land that surrounded the present-day city of Albany and was situated on both sides of the Hudson River. The colony of Rensselaerswyck and the West India Company officials had long been involved in disputes over jurisdiction of territory around the Fort. When the patroon of Rensselaerswyck claimed all land west of the Hudson River from Beeren Island to Moenemin's Castle (including Fort Orange) had been bought for him. The WIC claimed that the land around the Fort, which had been built six years prior to the patroonship, belonged to the WIC and was not included in the purchase of 1632.

Killiaen Van Rensselaer established a patroonship in the upper Hudson Valley in order to cultivate the land and mine the wilderness for farm and forest products that could be exported to Europe and sold. Before his death in 1643, he hired hundreds of willing pioneers from the Old World and sent them to Rensselaerswyck to be his tenants. These settlers consisted of farmers, artisans, tradesmen, and others who could support the new settlement. Most of Van Rensselaer's tenants settled within a few miles of Fort Orange.

On 10 April 1652, Director General Stuyvesant issued a proclamation. By this proclamation the main settlement of the Colony of Rensselaerswyck was removed from the jurisdiction of the patroon and created as an independent village called Beverwyck. Beverwyck later became Albany. The jurisdiction of the court included Fort Orange, Beverwyck, Schenectady, Kinderhook, Claverack, Coxsackie, Catskill and (until 1661) Esopus (present day Kingston). The Colony of Rensselaerswcyk was not included in this jurisdiction until 1665 when the two courts were ordered to combine.

Rensselaerswyck was the only one of five original Patroonships which was successful.

Fort Orange & Albany Beginnings

Fort Orange was the name given to the fur trading post built in 1624 on the west bank of the Hudson just south of the future site of Albany. The Dutch West India Company staffed the fort with employees to conduct business, kept a small detachment of soldiers to protect the outpost and maintain order, and brought in farmers (mainly French-speaking Walloons from Belgium) to provide food and other necessities. Some of these groups of settlers lived in small huts within the fort. Others lived outside the walls.

Some settlers came as family groups of husbands, wives, and children. Others (usually young men and boys) came individually. They were farmers and husbandmen, artisans and tradesmen, soldiers and clerks, labourers, and a few had more specialized training as surgeons, ministers, and skippers.

By the 1640s, fur traders had come together in a community north of the fort. This new settlement was given the name Beverwyck. The court of Fort Orange and the village of Beverwyck (present day Albany) was proclaimed by Stuyvesant in April of 1652. Settlers were attracted to Fort Orange by its location for Indian trade, but they were not always under the control of the Patroon of Rensselaerswyck. Fort Orange and the tiny hamlet that grew up outside its walls had been claimed by the Patroon as early as 1632, but this claim was argued by the West India Company and Stuyvesant. Governor Stuyvesant and Commissary Slichtenhorst were thus always in combat.

In April 10, 1652 the formation of the village of Beverwijck, established as the Court of Fort Orange and Beverwijck, temporarily resolved the dispute between the Patroonship of Rensselaerswyck and the West India Company. Until 1661 the powers of the magistrates of Fort Orange extended south to Esopus (Kingston) .

Fur Traders. Courtesy New York State Museum

The early population of Fort Orange and Beverwyck, while heavily Dutch, was changeable. Some settlers spent only a few years trading, then returned to Holland. Some retired to New Amsterdam (present day New York City), and others ventured further afield to the new lands at Kinderhook, Claverac, Catskill, Coxsackie, Niskayuna, Half Moon and Schenectady.

Needing land to raise food and other crops (such as tobacco), the Dutch soon looked further to western Long Island, a land much better suited for homesites. Soon, small villages cropped up -- New Utrecht, Breuckelen, both named after towns in the Netherlands, and Gravesend. Ferries plied the river between the settlement at New Amsterdam, on Manhattan Island, and the farming villages on Lange Eylandt (Long Island).

East on Court Street. Courtesy New York State Museum

Common Council, Albany. Courtesy New York State Museum

In March, 1664, the English King Charles II gave his brother, James, the Duke of York, a grant that covered the area from Maine south to the ``De la Ware Bay.'' James organized a fleet of warships under the command of Richard Nicolls. In late

August he anchored off the shoreline of Gravesend and threatened to attack Fort Amsterdam. Stuyvesant surrendered New Netherland on September 8th 1664 to this English invasion fleet. The Dutch agreed to leave, and James sent word of his victory to Massachusetts, signing his letter ``from New Yorke upon the Island of the Manhatoes.'' Nicolls became the first English governor of New Amsterdam and renamed it New York to honour the duke of York. Beverwyck became the village of Albany.

The Articles of Capitulation agreed to by the Dutch in 1664 were comparatively generous. Those Dutch settlers who wished to leave the colony were given 18 months in which to do so; those who chose to remain were required to take an oath of loyalty. The takeover also introduced a new element into Dutch customs - the sheriff of the county, clerk of the village and city, and officers and soldiers of the garrison who were mainly English or from New England. Many intermarried with the Dutch and became permanent citizens.

By the time of the English takeover in 1664, Fort Orange had been abandoned. Built by the lowland Dutch as a trading post, its riverside location made it susceptible to springtime flooding and unsuitable for its new purposes of protection under the English.

On August 9, 1673 the combined Dutch fleet of Cornelis Evertsz and Jacob Benckes captured New York. New York City was renamed New Orange; Kingston became Swanenburgh; Albany was named Willemstad; and Fort Albany became Fort Nassau. On November 10, 1674 the Treaty of Westminster officially returned New Netherland to England as the province of New York. The third Anglo-Dutch war had officially ended.

The Duke of York at first tried to maintain a detachment of soldiers in Albany to uphold his rights and keep the peace. After 1676, the Duke's government took a more determined approach to governing New York. In Dutch-speaking Albany, a new fort was built above the town, near the top of the main street leading from the river and connecting with the wilderness road that ran to Schenectady. The new Albany fort was not, as Fort Orange had been, a trading post. It was built to protect the settlers of the region while reminding them that now they were subjects of an English overlord. By the 1680s, the fort had two small buildings and was enclosed by a wooden stockade.

Fort Albany 1676. Courtesy New York State Museum

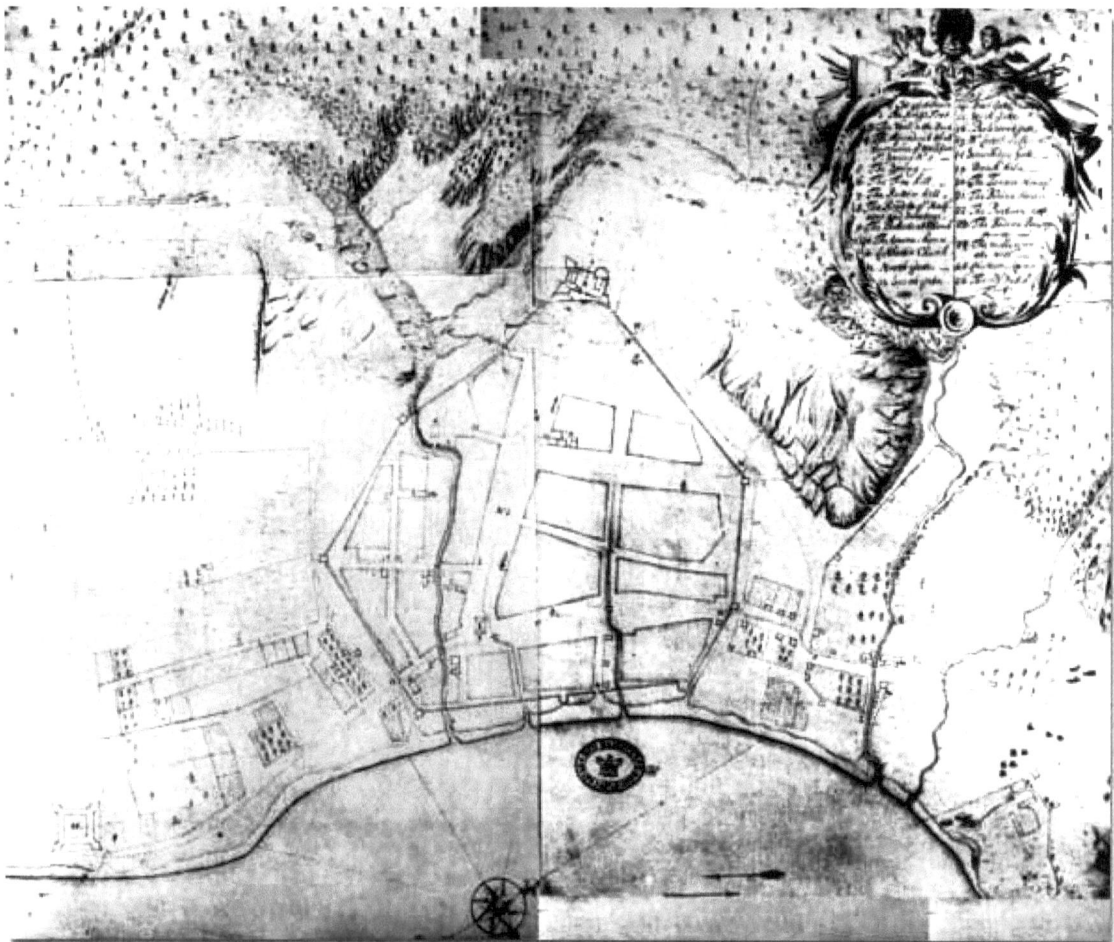

Overview of Fort Albany 1686. Roemer Map. New York State Museum

Albany County (not to be confused with the City of Albany) was one of the twelve original counties of colonial New York as established by Governor Thomas Dongan in 1683. Albany County was to "containe the Towns of Albany, the Collony Renslaerwyck, Schonecteda, and all the villages, neighborhoods, and Christian Plantacons on the east side of Hudson River from Roelof Jansen's Creeke, and on the west side from Sawyer's Creeke to the Sarraghtoga."

The Dongan charter of 1686 helped ease further tensions and questions of jurisdiction. Albany became a city on the river, one mile wide and 18.5 miles long. All settlements outside those limits belonged to the Colony.

By the division of the province into counties in 1688, Albany County consisted of all the territory north of Dutchess and Ulster Counties on both sides of the river. The village of Albany was considered the fountain of authority in both church and judicial matters.

Early Settlers & Immigration

What we call "passenger lists" were in reality account books of credits and debits for voyages. All such "passenger lists" for travel from The Netherlands to New Netherland between 1654 and 1664 are derived from information on the debit side of the West India Company Account Book. Thus the set of "passenger lists" that we have for the years 1654-1664 are from an account book showing who owed money when they arrived. The published lists draw only from the debit side; the credit side has not been published.

Typical fare for passage was 36 florins for each adult; half that for young children; and nothing for nursing infants. Names were not usually recorded except for the person owing the money. Thus we might see an entry such as "Cornelis Jacobszen van Beest, wife and two children ages 11 and 5" with an amount due beside the entry. The ages of children were given in order to determine the fee for passage.

A typical voyage from the Netherlands to New Netherland took between 7 and 8 weeks.

Many of the early shipping records from the West India Company have not survived, and we must use other records to determine who the early settlers were and when they arrived in the colony. One of these is the 1651 Oath of Fidelity to the Patroon in Rensselaerswyck.

We can also consult the notarial records held in Amsterdam, Netherlands. Approximately 10% of the total notarial records have been indexed, and they hold a wealth of information. Most early settlers to New Netherland entered into a contract with their employer (the Patroon or the WIC or an established settler with money) before leaving for the New World. Many of these contracts can be found in the Amsterdam Notarial Records and include details such as origin of the settler, contract period (2 to 6 years), wages and other agreed-upon details, and sometimes the name of the ship the settler was to sail on. Even if the name of the ship is not given, the date of the contract is usually a good indicator of the sailing date, as the contracts were entered into shortly before the settler sailed. A search of Jaap Jacobs' list of ships sailing from the Netherlands to the New World (and back) can often provide a strong circumstantial case for an individual's being on board a specific ship.

Religion

The established church in the United Netherlands was the Reformed Church. In 1628 the Dutch West India Company sent the Reverend Jonas Michaelius as the first ordained minister to New Netherland. However, even before the arrival of Michaelius, Sebastiaen Jansz Kroll had been sent over in 1624 as a comforter of the sick. Although he began his duties in New Amsterdam, he was soon sent to Fort Orange, arriving there in 1628. The comforters of the sick were required to read prayers every morning and evening, as well as before and after meals, to instruct and comfort the sick, to exhort those who required or requested exhortation, and to read chapters from the Bible and sermons of an ordained minister. The comforters were empowered to baptize and marry, but could not administer Holy Communion. A special form of service was prepared for them to read.

After a few months at Fort Orange, Comforter Krol returned to the Netherlands to obtain a minister for New Netherland. However the settlement was not considered large enough to warrant a minister, and Bastien Krol returned to New Netherland with power to baptize and marry, provided he used the liturgy of the church in his services. When Governor Peter Minuit arrived in 1626 to take charge of the colony, he ordered that the settlement should center about the southern portion of Manhattan Island. Soon after Peter Minuit's order, Comforter Krol left Fort Orange to become the first comforter at New Amsterdam.

In 1632 the Patroon Kiliaen van Rensselaer gave instructions that settlers in the Colony of Rensselaerswyck should come together every Sunday and on holidays to read passages and chapters from the Bible. Brant Peele van Niekerck was authorized by van Rensselaer to read from the Bible.

The church founded at Albany in 1640 was the only one north of Esopus with a permanent ministry - other than Schenectady. All babies were baptised and their names entered in the Doop Boek, but sadly Albany's records are scanty prior to 1684. Many are lost completely. The population of Fort Orange is not known in this early period, but it was small. The first church built in 1648 was 84x19 feet, and consisted of only nine benches for those attending services. This church was still in use until 1656.

It was not until 1642 that Dominie Johannes Megapolensis was hired to preach in Rensselaerswyck. There was no church building, and it is not known where he held services. In 1649 Dominie Megapolensis was called from Rensselaerwyck (Albany) to assume charge at Manhattan. For the next year, his son-in-law, Dominie Grasmeer, conducted the Albany area services.

The Patroon's trading house on the west side of the Hudson River, had been turned into a church in March 1648. The dominie was an ordained minister of the Dutch Reformed Church sent by the church leadership in the Netherlands to minister to the Albany congregation. Dominie Gideon Schaets arrived in the Colony in July 1652 and was minister until his death in 1694. Both dominies (ministers) and Deacons (lay leaders) staffed the church. The Deacons were prominent Albany businessmen and officials.

In June 1656 the cornerstone of the new Dutch Reformed Church was laid. There are no known surviving registers from the church at Beverwyck/Albany before 1684.

Albany Dutch Reformed Church.
Courtesy New York State Museum

List of Ministers at the Albany Dutch Reformed Church

Johannes Megapolensis, Jr. 1642-52
Gideon Schaets, 1652-1691
Godefridus Dellius, 1683-1699
Johannes Nucella, 1699-1700
Johannes Lydius, 1700-1710
Petrus Van Driessen, 1712-1738
Cornelis Van Schie, 1733-1744
Theodorus Frielinghuysen,1746-59
Eilardus Westerlo, 1760-1790
John Bassett, 1787-1804
John B. Johnson, 1796-1802

Money & Money Substitutes in New Netherland

Native Indians did not use currency. Instead they collected oblong shells which they polished and cut into beads. The finished highly polished beads were often attached to clothing. They were used as necklaces, belts and frequently strung in rows. These lengths of shells called wampum were often given as gifts. All beads were made up of highly polished cylinders about 1/8 " diameter and ¼" long, drilled length-wise and strung on ropes of hemp or the tendons of animals. While the local area dictated what shells could be used, in general black beads came from the local clam, known as the quahaug; while white beads came from winkles or periwinkles.

Indian beads were known by a variety of names among the early colonists – wampum, wampom-peage, wampeage, peage (which referred to beads that were strung), and in some localities such as New Netherland, seawan or seawand. In general the Dutch called it seawan (which they used for all shelled money), the English wampum. For the Indians, wampum referred strictly to white beads. They called their black beads suckaubock. The colonists used what they considered the generic term of wampum to refer to both varieties.

In 1609 Hudson's men received strings of beads from local Indians. The first European to use these beads for barter was a Dutch fur trader named Jacob Eelckens. In 1622 Eelckens demanded a ransom for a Pequot sachem (chief) on Long Island. The wampum Eelckens was given brought him more furs in trade than conventional trade goods. Before long the West India Company, recognizing a good thing, had their agents purchase all the wampum they could and take it north to Fort Orange. There they used it to buy furs from the Mahicans. Almost overnight wampum was functioning like money.

When Dutch traders encountered wampum they adopted it as a money substitute. Although more convenient than commodity money several problems developed with the use of wampum. It had no intrinsic value, and anyone could collect some shells and produce their own currency. With no central minting operation the quality of these products was often substandard. Shopkeepers needed to keep a vigilant eye for inferior wampum but there was no legislation in place that allowed them to refuse poor quality beads. Further, the amount of wampum produced was unregulated, and this eventually caused an oversupply.

In New Netherland wampum was legislated at four beads to the stiver, which was the Dutch equivalent of the English penny. However, so many poor quality unstrung beads were put into circulation that in April 1641 a law was passed prohibiting the use of unpolished beads during the month of May. During that month these poorer beads would be accepted in payment of taxes but only if they were strung and then only at the discounted rate of six beads to the stiver. The problems continued, and in

May 1650 an ordinance was passed prohibiting the use of loose wampum. This law also further discounted poorly made wampum that circulated on string, so that they traded at the rate of eight beads to the stiver. As more and more wampum flooded the market the value of all beads declined.

In 1661 Director General Stuyvesant addressed the colonists' concern over the steady inflation of wampum. Much of it was "unpierced and half-finished, made of stone, bone, glass, shells, horn, nay even of wood, and broken". Huge quantities of this inferior wampum was being dumped in the colony by the English with the result that wages and cost of goods rose. Stuyvesant ordered that all wampum used as money must first be strung, and its value was fixed at six white or 3 black beads per stiver for high quality trade wampum, and eight white or four black beads per stiver for inferior quality.

Seawant, or unstrung beads, which had been prohibited from daily commerce in 1650, was still used for tax payments. As late as 1693 commuters on the New York and Brooklyn ferry could pay with either two pence in silver or eight stivers in wampum. The last recorded exchange of wampum as money was in New York in 1701.

Patronymics

The most common Dutch naming custom was that of patronymics, or identification of an individual based on his/her father's name. For example, Jan Albertszen is named after his father, Albert. Albertszen means son of a man named Albert. The patronymic was formed by adding -se, -sen, -szen and –sz.

The patronymic ending for women was formed by adding –s, or -sdr. Women were sometimes recorded under their husband's name, thus forming a husband-o-nymic of sorts. For example, Maria Goosens (Maria, daughter of a man named Goosen) was sometimes recorded as Maria Jans (Jans being the feminine version of her husband Steven Janszen's patronymic).

An individual could also be known by his place of origin. For example, Cornelis Antoniszen was known in some records as 'van Breuckelen', meaning 'from Breuckelen' (Breuckelen being a town in the Netherlands). The place-origin name could be a nationality, as in the case of Albert Andriessen from Norway, originator of the Bradt and Vanderzee families. He is entered in many records as Albert Andriessen de Noorman, meaning Albert, son of Andries, the Norseman (Norwegian).

An individual might be known by a personal characteristic, for e.g. Vrooman means a wise man; Krom means bent or crippled; De Witt means the white one. Maria Goosens was called Lange Mary (tall Mary) and is found as such in several records of the day. A fascinating example is that of Pieter Adriaenszen (Peter, son of Adriaen) who was given the nickname of Soo Gemackelyck (so easy-going) but was also known as Pieter Van Waggelen/Van Woggelum from his place of origin. His children adopted the surnames Mackelyck and Woglom.

Sometimes an occupation became the surname. For example Smit meant a (black)Smith; Schenck was a cupbearer, Metsalaer was a mason, Cuyper was a barrelmaker.

An individual might be known by many different 'surnames' - and entered in official records under these different names, making the search difficult unless you're aware of the names in use. For e.g. Cornelis Antoniszen mentioned above was known, and written of, under the following names:

Cornelis   Antoniszen
Cornelis Teuniszen (Teunis being the diminuitive of Antony)
Cornelis Antoniszen/Teuniszen van Breuckelen
Cornelis Antoniszen/Teuniszen Van Slicht (this is how he signed his name and was likely a hereditary family name based on an old place of origin)

Broer Cornelis (name given him by Mohawks and meaning "Brother Cornelis" in Dutch))

There were also differences over the generations. Albert's sons and daughters took the surname Bradt except for his son Storm, born on the Atlantic Ocean during the family's sailing to the New World. Storm adopted the surname Vanderzee (from the sea) and this is the name his descendants carry.

The Dutch were much slower in adopting surnames as we know them than the English. Patronymics ended, theoretically, some time around 1687 but not everyone followed the new guidelines.

You must also be aware of the diminutives of regular first names, because the patronymic might be formed from the normal name or its diminuitive. For e.g.:

Antonis	Theunis/Teunis
Matthys	Thys/Tice
Harmanus	Harman, Manus
Jacobus	Cobus
Nicolas	Claes
Denys	Nys
Bartolomeus	Bartol, Meese/Meus
Cornelis	Krelis, Kees

The Settlement of Recife Brazil

Recife, in the province of Pernambuco Brazil, started its existence at the mouth of the Capibaribe and Beberibe rivers in 1548 as a fishing settlement, but it soon grew and became the seat of government during the period when the Dutch occupied the North East region of Brazil.

Frustrated at not having found gold in Brazil the Portuguese began farming sugar cane in order to make colonization economically viable.

During the colonial period most of the sugar mills were concentrated in the North East region of Brazil and in 1535 the town of Olinda in Pernambuco was founded.

The wealth of the Brazilian North East was envied by the Dutch who invaded Pernambuco in 1630 and captured Olinda that same year. But the town was not easily defensible, and the Dutch soon burned and abandoned it, moving their settlement to the neighbouring marshes around the hamlet of Recife.

After the formation of the West India Company in 1621 the Dutch set their eyes on Salvador da Bahia de Todos os Santos, the most important town in Portuguese Brazil. The expedition for the conquest of Salvador da Bahia started in December 1623. The Dutch fleet arrived off Salvador in May 1624. They were joined by the Dutch troops who entered the town two days later. The Portuguese governor surrendered but the conquest was short lived. In April 1625, a Portuguese fleet sailed to Salvador and entered the town. On on 30 April 1625, the Dutch capitulated.

The second attempt began in the summer of 1629. This time the Dutch objective was Pernambuco, the sought-after sugar colony in Brazil.

The commander of the Dutch fleet arrived at Pernambuco on February 1630. By the next evening the Dutch were in possession of Olinda, only a few miles from Recife. By the first week of March Portuguese resistance was over and the Dutch were masters of Recife, Olinda and the island of Antonio Vaz.

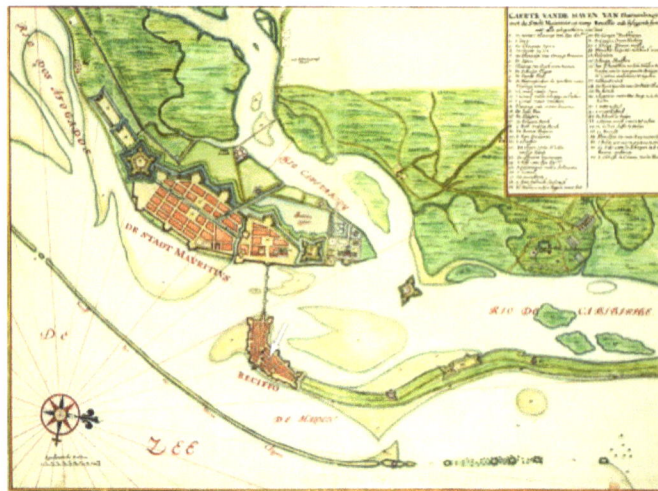
Mauritsstad and Recife 1643

The Portuguese governor Mathias de Albuquerque immediately organized a resistance. Some fortified camps were built around Recife, the most important one only about three miles from the town. For the next few years the Dutch and Portuguese attempts to capture each other's towns and forts continued.

At the beginning of 1636, reinforced by 2500 men from Portugal, the Portuguese again attacked. They advanced on Porto Calvo but its Dutch commander evacuated the town. The conquest of Porto Calvo gave the Portuguese the possibility to carry out many raids against Pernambuco that made settlement unsafe for the Dutch.

The Dutch subjects in Brazil were divided into two categories. The first were those employed by the WIC (soldiers, bureaucrats, Calvinist ministers). The second group were settlers, merchants, artisans, and tavern keepers. Many of these were ex-soldiers who had married and settled down but there were also settlers who had emigrated from the Netherlands to seek a new life in Nieuw Holland. The total white civilian population was about 3000.

The Dutch control on Brazil was always tenuous, and the WIC failed in its aim of colonization. The Dutch continued to lose their settlements and by the end of 1645 they possessed only Recife and the nearby Forts of Cabedello (Paraibá) and Ceulen (Rio Grande do Norte), as well as the islands of Itamaracá and Fernando de Noronha.

In November 1646 Fort Maurits was reoccupied by the Dutch but the following April the fort was abandoned. In February 1647 a Dutch expedition occupied the island of Itaparica in the Bay of Todos os Santos. In December 1647 the Dutch evacuated Itaparica. A new Dutch fleet under Witte de With left Holland the day after Christmas 1647 and arrived at Recife in March 1648.

In April 1648 a Dutch squadron of 5000 men under Commander Von Schoppe attacked the Portuguese forces and achieved some success. However the next day the Portuguese with only 2200 men launched an attack at the Guararapes that was an overwhelming victory. Soon the Portuguese reoccupied Olinda.

The Dutch at Recife were again besieged. At the end of 1648 the Dutch forces in Brazil totaled about 6000 white men and 600 Amerindians. In February 1649 a Dutch force of 3500 men occupied the Guararapes. The Portuguese marched against them with a force of 2600 men and the subsequent battle was an overwhelming victory for the Portuguese.

In February 1650 the situation of the Dutch at Recife, closely besieged by land, was very precarious, and the 3000 man garrison was demoralized. There were about 8000 civilians, of which roughly 3400 were the group made up of settlers, merchants, artisans, and tavern keepers, 600 were Jewish and 3000 to 4000 were Amerindians or blacks. The shortage of food and provisions was the worst enemy. The strength of the garrisons of Nieuw Holland was only about 4000 men.

On 20 December 1653 a Portuguese fleet of 77 ships appeared off Recife. The depots of the town were full of provisions but the garrison was unprepared to offer resistance. Just one month later, on 22 January 1654 the Dutch asked for terms of surrender, and on 26 January the capitulation was signed. Not only Recife but all territories still in Dutch hands were included. The Portuguese made their triumphal entry into Recife on 28 January 1654. [1]

The Dutch were given three months in which either to depart or to embrace the Roman Catholic religion and become Portuguese citizens. In April 1654, a fleet of sixteen Dutch ships sat at anchor in the Harbour of Recife ready to evacuate the Dutch Protestants together with a small number of Dutch and Portuguese Jews.

Fifteen of the ships arrived safely in the Netherlands, however, the sixteenth was captured by Spanish pirates only to be overtaken by the St. Charles, a French privateer. After much negotiating, the master of the St. Charles agreed to bring a group of twenty-three Jewish men, women and children from the captured ship to New Amsterdam for 900 guilders in advance and 1,600 on arrival.

In September 1654, the French ship St. Charles arrived in New Amsterdam these 23 Jews who had fled from Brazil. A petition by Jacques de la Motthe, the master of the ship, requested payment for Jews and their freight which he brought to New Amsterdam from Cape St. Anthony. He stated there were "23 souls, big and little, who must pay equally." de la Motte stated that "the Netherlanders who came over with them" were not included in his suit and that they had paid him. This means we have no record of who was on board but it is entirely possible that Hans Coenradt Barheit was one of the passengers. Asser Levy, a Jewish settler, was on board the St. Charles and he later acted as attorney in a 1658 suit against Hans Coenradt. [2]

Part II: The Immigrant Ancestor Hans Coenradt Barheit & his Wife Barentje Straetsman

The Barheit Lineage

Several Barheit siblings were mentioned in Jonathan Pearson's "Genealogies of the First Settlers of Albany" but no attempt was made to document their parents. All that has been known about the family is that the siblings used the patronymic Hanse and thus their father's first name was Hans.

Briefly, Pearson mentions the siblings Jeronimus Hanse Barheit and Andries Hanse Barheit, their wives and children [3], but he speaks of Andries Hanse (Scherp) as "perhaps" being the same individual as Andries Hanse (Barheit). However they are two distinct individuals and in fact there is a third Andries Hanse (Andries Hanse Huyck) in the same area at the same time.

Pearson mentions other Barheit males with their wives and children but no attempt was made to assign these individuals to complete family groups. Johanna Hanse Barheit is mentioned but only as the spouse of Pieter Willemse Van Slyke under the Van Slyke section of the book, and without her patronymic of Hanse [4].

My research into church records in Recife (formerly Pernambuco) Brazil, court documents in Albany and other miscellaneous records reveals more information on the Barheit family. Conclusions can be drawn from studying the naming patterns of children of the Barheit siblings and my intent in this book is to demonstrate the family group as I have determined it from my studies.

It is important to note that naming patterns of children can help determine family groups – the Dutch very often named their first two sons after the paternal and maternal grandfathers, and their first two daughters after the paternal and maternal grandmothers (not necessarily in that order).

Baptismal sponsors can also help determine family groups. The Dutch liked to use family members for this important role. If no family were available, friends would be called on to fill the role. The first thing I did was to check the names of the children of the Barheit siblings and possible siblings. Then I checked the baptismal sponsors to see how or if they were related.

The results confirmed my theory, that there were six Barheit siblings – Anna Maria Hanse Barheit who married Jan Spoor aka Wiberse; Anna Darber [Barber?] Hanse, no further information; Johanna Hanse Barheit who married Pieter Willemse Van Slyke; Jeronimus Hanse Barheit who married Rebecca Evertse; Andries Hanse Barheit who married Geertje Teunise; and Johannes Hanse Barheit who married first Catharina Gilbert and secondly Catalyna Dingman.

Further research into Recife Brazil records, Albany Court Records and other documents suggest that the parents of these six Barheit siblings were Hans Coenradt, a baker in Albany as early as 1654, and his wife Barentje Straetsman.

We know from court documents of May 1684 in Albany that Barentje Straetsman had five surviving children by her husband Hans Coenradt. [5]

While Hans Coenradt is not found in records under the surname Barheit this is not unusual. Surnames were often not found in the New Netherland community until after 1684 at which point children of the immigrant ancestor are often recorded with a surname.

Hans is found in various records in Brazil, Amsterdam and New Netherland as Hans de baker (Hans the baker), Hans Coenradt (Hans son of Coenradt), Hans Coenraets van Neurenburch (Has Coenradt from Nuremburg) and Hans Coenradt van Beerhey (Hans Coenrdat from Beerhey [6]). This is the only clue we have as to how the Barheit surname came into use. I suggest that Beerhey is the surname the children of Hans Coenradt eventually used, and that it was phonetically represented as Barheit.

A look at the names of the children of the five Barheit siblings reveals that the mother Barentje Straetsman was honoured by having grand-daughters named after her. Three of Barentje's children named daughters in her honour. Johannes Barheit, Johanna Barheit Van Slyke, and Anna Maria Barheit Spoor each named a daughter Barentje. The other two siblings only had one daughter each so did not have an opportunity to honour their mother. Jeronimus Barheit appears to have only had one daughter before his death so not naming a daughter Barentje is not an indication that he didn't have a mother with that name. Andries Barheit also had only one daughter but he did name one of his sons Barent, the male equivalent of Barentje.

The chapters on each of the Barheit siblings will help explain my findings, and the charts for their children and baptismal sponsors will show the relationship of baptismal sponsors to the parents, and to each other.

Hans Coenradt & Barentje Straetsman in Brazil

The first reference found of Hans Coenradt having lived in Brazil is in court records dated 23 July 1658 in Fort Orange. Asser Levy acted as the attorney for Joseph d'Acost (the plaintiff) against Hans Coenradt (the defendant) for money due to the plaintiff from the defendant. [7] Judgement had been previously given in favour of the plaintiff in the Court of Justice in Recife Brazil.

Hans admitted he owed the money but stated that he "was driven out of Brazil by the enemy" from which we know that Hans fled when Brazil fell from Dutch power to the Portuguese in 1654.

The plaintiff argued that Hans was ordered to pay cash, in pieces of eight, one year before Recife fell to the Portuguese and he maintains that Hans must still pay in either pieces of eight, in beavers, or in any other currency in use in New Netherland. The court ordered Hans to pay. [8]

Since this record revealed the Recife connection, I searched the published church baptism records for Recife [9] and found Hans and his wife Barentie both baptising their own children, and standing as sponsors for other couples' baptising children. Barentje Straetsman's sister Teuntie [10] was in Recife at the same time, having married first Hans Meyers, a trumpeteer in the Army, secondly Juriaen Haff, and baptising children by both husbands in the church in Recife.

Hans Coenraats is found as a sponsor at several baptisms in the Recife church from March 1644 to July 1650. Thus we can place Hans in Recife Brazil by March 1644. We know however from court records in Albany that Hans had a house and land granted to him 27 March 1643 by Governor Maurits on the neighbouring island of Antonio Vaz in the town of Mauritsstad. Hans' house was in the marketplace of Mauritsstad, and one side was next to the "old kitchen" of the Governor. [11] It appears that Hans was living in Mauritsstad, which was on an island off the coast of Recife, and thus may not have come ashore to baptise all his children born during his stay in Brazil. Placing Hans in Brazil as early as 1643 and knowing that the Dutch settlers fled in April 1654 means that Hans and Barentje lived in the Recife area for approximately ten years.

Following is a list of babies for whom Hans Coenradt acted as sponsor:

31 Mar. 1644. no name. Farns Carsel en Hilleken --- Get [sponsors]: Hans Coenraed
31 Mar. 1646. no name. Frans Kessel en Celijken Kessels. get: Hans Coenraets
19 Dec. 1647. Dirck. Ouders [parents] Dirck Symonss en Janneken Willems. get; Hans Coenraets, Jan Evertss, Martha Henricx
20 Sept. 1648. Johannes. Ouders Hans Cleyn en Cathrina Steerekints. get: Hans Counraet in plaats van de vader [Hans Coenraets in place of the father], Pieter Willems, Geertien Calckers

30 June 1649. Laurens en Pieter. Ouders Jurriaen haeff en Teuntien Meyerinck. get Hans Coenract [brother in law of Teuntie, the mother, who was the sister of Barentje Straetsman], Pieter de Mee, Lucas Beucker, hans Vogelhooft

17 Oct. 1649. Poulus. Ouders Dirck Pouluss en Henrickie Pouluss. get Hans Coenraets, Wijnant Roeloffs, Hesther van Ravesteyn

14 Nov. 1649. Hans. Ouders Adam Hansen en Maria Henricx. get Pieter Seegers, Hans Counraets, Maria Henricx

2 Jan 1650. Counraet en Henrick Frederick. Ouders Joost Stadelaer en Margarita Stadelaer. Get Hans Counraet, Henrick Heerzeele, Martha Helt

6 July 1650. Johannes. Ouders Leenaerd Clasen en Hilletie Janssen. get Hans Counraets, Margrieta Backs, Elsie Stuete

In 1650 and 1651 Hans and his wife Barentje baptised their first two daughters in this same church in Recife.

14 Dec. 1650. Anna Darber [sic but probably should be Anna Barber]. Ouders: Hans Coenraet en Barentge Straetmans. get Dirck Pauwels, Grisella Lits

22 Dec. 1651. Anna Mary. Ouders Hans Coenraet en Barentje Jans. get Jacob Scherff, Maria Hendricx

Here we learn Barentje Straetsman's father's name (Jan) as she is recorded with her patronmyic of Jans.

No marriage record for Hans Coenradt and Barentje Straetsman has been found. However we know that they were married as early as July 1649, for on that date Barentje was recorded with her husband-o-nymic [12] of Coenradt, when she stood as sponsor for Annetie the daughter of Jan Dircksen and Annetie Dircks.

31 July 1649. Annetie. Ouders Jan Dircksen en Annetie Dircks. get Claes Meyer, jacques Vallot, Barentie Counraets, Barbara Sickes

Barentje is found in Brazil as early as October 1643. Whether she came as a married woman with her husband Hans Coenradt, or met and married Hans in Recife is not known. Since we find her in the church records in 1643, we can assume she was at least 16 at the time she acted as sponsor, and most likely she was closer to 21 years or older. It appears that her first child was born in 1647 when she would most likely be between 20 and 25. This gives us an estimated birth year for Barentje of 1622.

We find Barentje recorded in 1643 with her patronymic of Jans at the baptism of the child of Hans Cleen and Maria Stock.

14 Oct. 1643. no name. Ouders Hans Cleen en Maria Stock. get Johannes Becker, Jan Willems, Barentie Janss

She is found once more acting as baptismal sponsor in 1651.

18 Oct. 1651. Janne. Ouders Piere la Heere en Clasijn Frederick. get Jan Elbertsen, Barentie Straetman

After Hans and Barentje fled Recife Brazil, they probably sailed to Amsterdam in the fleet of ships sent to rescue the settlers there. Many of the Brazil settlers remained in Amsterdam or other parts of the Netherlands but some continued on to the thriving colony of New Netherland. The first record found indicating Hans was in New Netherland is dated in Albany (Fort Orange) in early December 1655. So sometime between April 1654 and December 1655, Hans (and probably his entire family) arrived in New New Netherland.

Barentje and two children left Amsterdam 22 December 1659 or after 8 January 1660 on board de Trouw with Captain Jan Jansz Bestevaer. Presumably this was a second trip for Barentje and not her first arrival in the colony, as she is mentioned in court records in New Amsterdam in 1658. The ship arrived in New Amsterdam before 6 June 1660. Barentje is recorded on the list of money due for passage as:

"The wife of Hans Coenradt, baker at Fort Orange, and two children 7 and 12 years old "

From this record we know that there were two children born circa 1647 and circa 1652. The name of the 12 year old is not known with certainty [13], but the 7 year old child was most probably Anna Maria baptised 1651 in Recife Brazil. Little Anna Darber [sic], baptised the year before her sister Anna Maria, was most likely deceased.

Hans Coenradt & Barentje Straetsman in New Netherland

The exact date of Hans Coenradt's arrival in New Netherland is not known but we know he would have been among the refugees fleeing Recife Brazil in April 1654. Presumably the family continued on to New Netherland soon after arriving safely in the Netherlands. The first record found indicating he was in New Netherland is dated in Albany (Fort Orange) in early December 1655. [14] So sometime between April 1654 and December 1655, Hans (and probably his entire family) arrived in New New Netherland.

As New Amsterdam came into view with its gallows and weather beaten wooden houses dominating a raw, windswept landscape, the Barheit family must have had mixed feelings. New Amsterdam in 1654 was a frontier outpost filled with brawling sailors and rough-looking fur traders. Over fifty grog houses catered to a never-ending stream of men dropping in for a little fun on their way to or from Massachusetts or Virginia. [15]

Many researchers believe that Barentje stayed behind in the Netherlands and arrived in New Netherland for the first time in 1660. Records reveal that Barentje and two children left Amsterdam between 22 December 1659 and 8 January 1660 on board the ship de Trouw. The ship sailed into the harbour at New Amsterdam some time before 6 June 1660. [16] However it is unlikely that this was her Barentje's first trip, since it occurred at least five years after her husband's arrival. Barentje more than likely returned to the Netherlands on either business reasons or to visit family, and this 1660 arrival is her return voyage.

We find records of Barentje in New Netherland as early as August 1658 when she was called a whore by Pieter Jansen. Her sister defended her vigourously and Pieter took her sister to court in New Amsterdam. [17] This suggests that the 1660 voyage was not her first time to New Netherland.

The late Pim Nieuwenhuis' abstracts from notarial documents in the Amsterdam Archives reveal that on 16 August 1659, Barentje was in Amsterdam conducting business on behalf of her sister Teuntje. [18] It seems obvious that Barentje, her legal affairs in order, then booked passage on the next ship to New Netherland – de Trouw leaving after 22 Decemember 1659.

This abstract is the only clue we have as to how the Barheit name came into use, as it states that Barentje's husband was "Hans Coenraets from Beerhey". I suggest that Beerhey is the surname the family eventually used, phonetically represented as Barheit.

The Barheit family may have found themselves in financial difficulty in New Netherland. The WIC owed Hans back pay for his time spent as a soldier. He left everything behind when he and his family fled Brazil after the Portuguese took control in 1654.

In 1657 Hans approached the Albany courts to appoint Jan van Eeckelen of Beverwyck to obtain the moneys due to him (Hans) from the WIC for his services as a soldier in that company. [19] This appears not to have been successful for in 1660 Hans appointed his wife Barentje to act on his behalf to obtain the money he was owed. [20] It may be that Hans was in failing health, for we are left to puzzle over why he appointed Barentje, why did he not pursue the matter of his missing wages personally?

Financial difficulties also struck when he fled from Brazil in 1654, for Hans lost the house and land in the town of Mauritsstad granted to him 11 years earlier by Governor Maurits. His attempt in 1663 to be compensated for that loss may also have been unsuccessful.[21]

1659 saw Hans Coenradt in court suing his former partner Jan van Eeckelen. Hans claimed that when their partnership dissolved, they made a contract and he now wants that contract honoured. Jan offered to pay 63 schepels of wheat to Hans. [22] In May 1660 the wife of Klaes Jansen took Hans to court and sued him over a debt of two beavers. The court ordered Hans to pay. [23]

Then Barentje's sister and only known relative, Teuntje Straetsmans, who lived at Gowanus, died on 19 October 1662. When the deacons inventoried Teuntje's estate six days later, they found a large supply of vegetables which they packed up and sent to Barentje.

> "sent to Barentje Straetsman wife of hans de Backer, living at Fort Orange, to be sold on behalf of the deceased- 155 Pumpkins, 55 Waterlemons [24], 200 Beetroots, 33 Calabashes [25], 5 1/2 schepels of onions" [26]

In October 1669 Barentje found herself in the Albany courts, being sued by Geertruyt Barents (wife of Jacob Heven) for the remainder of house rent due in beavers, and more than six months back money for rent. Barentje admitted she owed the money but claimed Geertruyt failed to make promised repairs on the house she was in. Arguments continued, with Geertruyt telling the court she sold the house to Barentje and thus did not have to make repairs. As well, stated Geertruyt, she ended up being forced to keep the house but had expenses in connection with the sale. The court ordered Barentje to pay the remainder of rent due (fl 140) but denied Geertruyt her claim for six months back rent because the promised repairs had not been made. Barentje was in luck because the courts further ordered Geertruyt to "vacate the premises immediately". [27]

Barentje and Hans fell on hard times and from March 1672 until Hans' death in January1674 had to rely on the Deacons of the Reformed Church in Albany for help.

In March 1672 the deacons of the Albany Reformed Church gave Barentje a mudde [28] of grain worth f16. [29] Barentje is often noted in the accounts as being given handouts for her family and for Hans over the next two years.

The handouts included sums of money [30], wheat [31], soap [32], clothing and material [33], shoes [34], butter [35], sugar [36], salt, wine and beer [37], blankets, bear skins, pillows, hired labour to build a cooking oven [38], candles [39], venison [40], and the pall for Hans' funeral.

By 18 January 1674 Hans was dead and the Deacons of the Church gave Barentje a sheet to use for his funeral pall. [41] Less than two weeks later on 31 January the last entry concerning Barentje and Hans is found in the deacon's list of accounts – for 4 schepels of wheat to Hans de backer's widow. [42]

Barentje was left an impoverished widow with five children, the oldest about 23 years of age, the youngest about 12. By September of 1674 she had remarried to the widower Jacob Janse Gardenier aka Flodder whose wife Josyna had died in February 1669 leaving him with ten children.

Barentje Straetsman & Jacob Janse Gardenier aka Flodder

Barentje's poverty may have influenced her hasty second marriage just a few months after the death of Hans Coenradt in January 1674. Left a widow in her early 50's (if we assume a birth year of about 1622) with five children, a quick marriage would be one of the few ways Barentje could survive.

We see some evidence that her new husband was busy paying off her debts. In a court document dated 3 July 1678 in Albany, Jacob gave a bond to pay arrears of rent owed by his wife Barentje Straetsman to none other than Geertruy Barents, wife of Jacob Hevick – the same woman Barentje owed rent to some ten years earlier. The rent owed was 168 gl, which Jacob promised to pay in installments, the first being a payment of 21 beavers due in May 1679. On 30 July 1680 Geertruy signed her acceptance of payments made in full. [43]

Albany County Deeds records a lengthy agreement between Jan Jacobse Gardenier, one of Jacob Janse's sons, and his step-mother Barentje Straetsman.

"…between Jan Gardenier eldest sonne [sic] of the deceased Jacob Gardenier empowered and representing all the rest of his brethren and sisters being in all nine besides himself, and Barentje Straetsman widow and relict of the said Jacob Janse Gardenier deceased, having five children procreated by her husband Hans Coenrats concerning certain Testamentary Disposition between her and her last husband made by Robert Livingston and dated the 13th day of May 1684.

First wee [sic] understan and award that the said widow Barentje Straetsman shall remain and keep possession of the whole Estate so long as she lives or til such time as she remarries, as herefater further is declared, but withall obliged to deliver a true inventory of the estate to the eldest sonne Jan Gardenier, and put two sufficient suretyes that she shall well administer upon the estate.

Secondly that she is to have honest overseers, of which she may choose one and the other must be chosen by the said Jan Gardenier that the estate may be justly and well administered.

Thirdly that the ten children of the deceased Jacob Janse Gardenier, who have had no cow and hogge [sic] as yet, shall have the same out of the estate

Fourthly if it should happen that the said widow should be pressed by the creditors for the payment of the debts of her said deceased husband Jacob Gardenier and he constrained to sell cattle, Neger [sic] or Negroes, then is suh case the said Jan Gardenier shall have the preference; he paying as much for the same as another would be willing to give

Fifthly the land lying upon Schotak with what dependeth theron, said widow may make use of or let to farm as long as she lives but my not Burthen or allienate the same, except toward the payment of the dbets made before the decease of her said husband Jacob Gardenier. If the other estate (so as the same is now) be not sufficient for the payment of the same.

Sixthly after the decease of the said widow the said land is not what dependeth theron shall be apprized by indifferent men but the said Jan Garednier shall be preferred… the sale which many shall be divided in fifteen parts each child a parte and part.. to wit ten parts to the children of Jacob Gardenier deceased and five parts to the children of the widow Barentje Straetsman.

Seventhly concerning the other estate and goods if she should depart this life a widow (all debts being paid), shall be divided in the manner or way as on the 6th article set forth but if she should remarry then the estate shall be divided so as the estate…then… be found… in two equal shares, to wit – said one half or moyety to said widow and the other half for the ten children of the deceased Jacob Gardenier each child part and part alike.

Eighthly if it should fall out (God forbid) that the widow should have great occasion and by poverty be neessitate in the time of widowhood to sell some of the said estate and good come of deceased party (the land excepted) she may do it, for her alimentation and necessary payment, but not otherwise, always provided it be with the knowledge and approbation of the said overseers who are bound in conscience to consider the case aright.

Ninethly that herewith is mortified and disannulled all pretensions of the ten children of Jacob Gardenier, concerning their deceased Mother's estate and all whatever may depend theron

Tenthly that the parties on both sides with what award is made above be at quiet and rest or he that doth otherwiseis first obligated to pay fifty pounds current money of this province according to their fee and voluntary engagement made (among others) with the presence of William Nicolls and Robert Livingston, and for said binding same did exchange a Ryall.

Signed Hendrick Van Nes, Jan Becker, Albany 156 March 1687/88. " [44]

Part III: The Second Generation – the Children of Hans Coenradt Barheit & Barentje Straetsman

Johanna Hanse Barheit and her husband Pieter Willemse Van Slyke

The Van Slykes of Coxsackie, New York, descend from Pieter Willemse Van Slyke, who was probably born in Beverwyck or Kinderhook circa 1660 to 1664.

Pieter Willemse may have been the eldest son of Willem Pieterse Van Slyke and his wife Baertie. In keeping with Dutch customs, the first two sons were usually named in honour of their grandparents. Since Pieter was named in honour of his paternal grandfather (Pieter Antonissen Van Slyke, the brother of Cornelis), he was probably the first or second son. His marriage to Johanna Hanse Barheit is found in the Albany Reformed Dutch Church on 9 April 1684. [45] Given the average Dutch marriage ages for men we can estimate he was between 20 and 25 years old on this date. This gives us an estimated birth year of 1659 to 1664 but because his father did not arrive in the colony until 1660 we can narrow that to 1660 to 1664. In previously published works, the only information given for his wife Johanna has been that she was the daughter of a man named Hans (based on her patronymic of Hansen) and used the surname Barheit (found in baptismal records of her children). Thus researchers have concluded that she was the daughter of an unknown Hans Barheit.

However I have found evidence which indicates that Johanna was almost certainly the daughter of Hans Coenradt and his wife Barentje Straetsman of Fort Orange and Albany. Hans had been a soldier in Recife Brazil, but after the fall of Recife to the Portuguese in 1654, he came to New Netherland as a baker. He settled in Fort Orange with his wife Barentje Straetsman. It is interesting to note that Barentje Straetsman and two children arrived in 1660 on the same ship that Willem Pieterse Van Slyke sailed on as a 19 year old. [46]

On 30 September 1674, Barentje Straestman, newly married to Jacob Janse Gardenier, aka Flodder, bound her 8 year old daughter Johanna Hans to Richard and Elizabeth Pretty, for a period of 8 years. The indenture names Hans Coenradt as Johanna's father. [47] I suggest this Johanna Hans is the same Johanna Hans who became the wife of Pieter Willemse Van Slyke, and whose siblings later assumed the Barheit surname. We must remember that surnames were not in general use in Dutch families until after 1674, and the early New Netherland records can be confusing as individuals switch between patronymics, surnames, nicknames and a wide variety of spelling variations. We must use clues to determine if individuals named in records are different or the same person. Much evidence points to this Johanna Hans, daughter of Hans Coenradt and Barentje Straetsman, being Johanna Hans Barheit, wife of Pieter Willemse Van Slyke. One of the more important clues in determining relationships is to examine the baptismal sponsors used at the births of a couples' children.

The Dutch tended to use family members as sponsors at children's baptisms, and if no family member was close at hand, the parents turned to friends or people who had some importance to them. The task of being a sponsor was not something taken lightly. Therefore it is always wise to search the baptismal sponsors carefully to try to determine their relationships with the couple. The early Albany Church baptisms use the word "by" in front of the sponsor name to record who held the baby, a very important role.

A second important clue to determining family relationships is the use of traditional Dutch naming patterns. If Pieter and Johanna followed these traditional naming patterns, their first two sons should be named in honour of the grandfathers, their first two daughters in honour of the grandmothers.

The following list showing the baptisms of Pieter Willemse and Johanna Han's nine known children illustrates the naming patterns followed, and the relationships of the baptismal sponsors to the parents. (Johanna Hans Barheit and Pieter Willemse Van Slyke)

Date of Baptism; Child's Name; Baptismal Sponsors
- 20 Sept 1685; Willem; Willem Neefie, Barentje Neefie *(parents of Pieter Willemse Van Slyke)*
- 25 Sept 1687; Hans; Hieronimus Hansz, Rebecca Everts *(brother & sister in law of Johanna Hans Barheit)*
- 2 Feb. 1690; Lysbeth; Leendert Arentsz , Elizabeth Pritty *(Elizabeth Pretty, wife of Sheriff Richard Pretty, the woman to whom Barentje Straetsman bound her daughter Johanna Hans as a servant in 1674)*
- 20 nov 1692; Teunis; Jan Hansz *(probably Johanna's brother Johannes Hanse Barheit)* , Elsje Rutgersz
- 26 May 1695; Johanna (Anna); Hendrik Van Dyk , Jannetje Swart
- 14 Nov. 1697; Tryntje; David Schuyler , Elsje Staats
- 28 Apr. 1700; Pieter; Cornelis Van Ness, Marritje Van Ness
- 3 Jan. 1703; Barentje; Lambert Huyck , Rachel Dingemans *(Rachel was the step-granddaughter of Barentje Straetsman by her marriage to Jacob Janse Gardenier aka Flodder, and step-niece to Johanna)*
- 28 Oct. 1705; Dirck; Pieter Van Brug , Grietje Barheit *(Grietje was another niece to Johanna and daughter of Johanna's brother Jeronimus Hanse Barheit)*

Pieter and Johanna's naming of a son Hans and a daughter Barentje appears to have been in honour of the maternal grandparents Hans Coenradt and Barentje Straetsman. The son Willem was no doubt in honour of Pieter's father Willem Pieterse Van Slyke. That there is no daughter named Beertje in honour of Pieter's mother Baertje may be a matter of there having been an earlier child named Beertje who died or whose baptism was not recorded. Another child could have been born between the baptisms of Lysbeth in February 1690 and Teunis in November 1692 or Teunis and Johanna in May 1695. Or Pieter and his mother may have been estranged and thus no child named after her.

Johanna's daughter Lysbeth baptised in 1690 was no doubt named in honour of Elizabeth Pretty, wife of Sheriff Richard Pretty. Richard and Elizabeth had no children of their own, and it is not unreasonable to expect that they may have become quite fond of the little 8 year old, Johanna Hans, who lived with them until the age of 16. This explains the important role filled by Elizabeth Pretty at the baptism of Lysbeth, where she held the child who was her namesake. Johanna's naming of a daughter Lysbeth (the short form of Elisabeth) in Elizabeth Pretty's honour would be expected.

From the baptisms found in the Albany church records we can see a pattern emerge. I suggest that the children of Pieter and Johanna's may have been named after the following relatives:

- Willem – named in honour of Pieter's father Willem Pieterse Van Slyke
- Hans - named in honour of Johanna's father Hans Coenradt (Barheit)
- Lysbeth - named in honour of Elizabeth Pretty with whom Johanna lived from age 8 to 16
- Teunis - named in honour of Pieter's brother Teunis Willemse Van Slyke
- Johanna (Anna) – unknown or possibly named after Johanna herself
- Tryntje - named in honour of Pieter's sister Tryntje Willemse Van Slyke
- Pieter - named in honour of Pieter's grandfather Pieter Antonissen Van Slyke or after Pieter himself
- Barentje - named in honour of Johanna's mother Barentje Straetsman[48]
- Dirck - named in honour of Pieter's brother Dirck Willemse Van Slyke

On June 8, 1703 a certificate of the election of Pieter Vosburgh, Lammert Janse and Pieter Verslyke [sic], as Trustees of the town of Kinderhook, was filed at Albany. This is probably the same Peter Van Slyck who along with Derick van der Carr, was elected trustee "by and for the inhabitants of the township of Kinderhook" on 12 June 1703. [49]

Pieter died circa January 1741/42, having left a will which he wrote in 1735. It was probated 16 January 1741/42. In it he names his children, and since he provides Teunis with more than the others "in right of primogeniture" we know that Teunis is now the eldest living son. Willem and Hans, who were baptised before Teunis, are dead.

Will of Pieter Willemse Van Slyke: In the name of God, Amen, March 25, 1735. I, PETER VAN SLYKE, of Keyserick, [Kinderhook] in Albany County, being in health. If my wife survives me she shall dispose of all that remains of my estate according to her pleasure. I leave to my son Theunis, 1 good cow in his right of primogeniture. I leave to Barentie Barhuyt, "for that she hath served me," £10. To my son Dirck, 2 negroes. I leave all the rest of my estate to my seven children, Thomas [50], Peter, Dirck, Elizabeth, wife of Arie Gardiner, Catharine, wife of Moses Ingersoll, Anna, wife of John Jacob Ral [51], and Barentie. I make my sons executors.

Witnesses, A. Van Dyke, Lambert Hyck, Joshua Hyck. Proved, January 16, 1741/2.
End of Liber 13 [52]

Johannes Hanse Barheit & his wives Catharina Gilbert & Catalyna Dingman

The following list showing the baptisms of Johannes Hanse Barheit's nine known children by his two wives will illustrate the naming patterns followed, and the relationships of the baptismal sponsors to the parents

Date of Baptism; Child's Name; Baptismal Sponsors

By wife #1 Catharina Gilbert daughter of John Gilbert & Cornelia Vandenburgh
- 16 May 1703; Johannes (after maternal grandfather); Jan Gilbert *(paternal grandfather)*, Albert Rykman, Cornelia Gilbert *(maternal grandmother)*
- 8 Oct 1706; Cornelia (after maternal grandmother); Gerrit Wibusse, Mary Wibbuse *(nephew of Johannes Hans Barheit & nephew's wife; also Barentje Straetsman's grandson)*
- 20 March 1709; Hieronimus (after Johannes' brother); Hieronimus Barheit, Rebecca Barheit *(brother and sister in law to Johannes Hanse Barheit)*
- 14 Oct. 1711; Barentje; Willem Gillebart, Cornelia Gillebart *(the maternal grandmother)*
- 10 Jul 1715; Willem; Willem Gilbert, Christina Cuylers
- 27 Aug 1715; Teunis; Balthus and Lidia Van Benthuisen

By wife #2 Catalyna Dingman daughter of Adam Dingman & Aaltje Jacobse Gardenier
- 25 Oct 1719; Alida (after Catalyna's mother); Cornelis Maasen *(son of Maas Cornelis married to Jacomyntje Jacobse Gardenier the sister of maternal grandmother; Barentje Straetsman's step-grandson)*, Anna Warms.
- 06 Oct 1723; Adam (after Catalyna's father); Claes Gardenier *(cousin to Catalyna Dingman; Barentje Straetsman's step-grandson)*, Rachel Gardenier
- 01 Oct 1725; Dirck?; Johann and Elyz. Bratt

Heronimus Hanse Barheit and his wife Rebecca Evertse

Heronimus (Jeronimus) Barheit married Rebecca Evertse in Albany. Their marriage was recorded in the Albany Reformed Church on 9 April 1684. Only two children's baptisms have been found for this couple – Margriet baptised in the same church on 4 October 1685 [53]and Wouter baptised six years later on 4 August 1691 [54].

Heronimus' will was written 22 August 1718 and proved 23 February 1722. In it he names his wife Rebecca, son Wouter and one daughter.

Anna Maria Hanse Barheit and her husband Jan Spoor aka Wibese

Jan Spoor aka Wibese (Wybesse, Wubuse) lived at Niskayuna. In 1662 Jan Wybesse Van Harlingen, a farm servant, bought 16 morgens of land at Catskill from Christoffel Davids. In 1698 he sold his land at Niskayuna to Johannes Schuyler for L120. [55]

Pearson does not give Jan's wife Anna Maria a surname, she is only referred to by her patronymic of Hanse. My research suggests she was the daughter baptised in Pernambuco (now Recife) Brazil to Hans Coenradt (Barheit)and Barentje Straetsman. Her baptismal record reads:

> Dec 22, 1653. Anna Mary. Hans Coenraet, Barentje Jans. Wit: Jacob Scherff, Maria Hendricx [56]

In this church record we see Barentje Straetsman's patronymic (Jan) and thus learn her father's name – Jan Straetsman.

The following chart showing the baptisms of Anna Hanse Barheit's children by her husband Jan Spoor aka Wibese will illustrate the naming patterns followed, and the relationships of the baptismal sponsors to the parents

Date of Baptism; Child's Name; Baptismal Sponsors
- ca 1676; Johannes/Jan/Hans *(named after Anna Maria's father, Hans Coenradt)*; No baptismal record
- ca 1680; Barentje *(named after Anna Maria's mother, Barentje Straetsman)*; No baptismal record
- before 6 Feb. 1690; Antje; No baptismal record
- 3 Dec. 1684; Saartje; Jacomyntje Maasz *(Jacomyntje Jacobse Gardenier, stepdaughterof Barentje Straetsman)*
- circa 1686; probably Gerrit; No baptismal record found
- 27 Apr 1690; Nicolaas; Pieterje Fransz (presenter of child), the father
- 7 June 1691; Annetje; Rebecca Douwe *(wife of Douwe Jellis Fonda. Her daughter Rebecca was the god-daughter of Aaltje Evertse, probable sister-in-law of Heronimus Hanse Barheit)*
- 22 April 1694;Rebecca; Maas Cornelisz *(married to Jacomyntje Jacobse Gardenier who was Barentje Straetsman's stepdaughter)*, Rebecca Everts *(married to Anna Maria's brother Heronimus Hans)*
- 31 Jan 1697; Rachel; Caspar Liendertsz *(Caspar Leendertsz Conyn husband of Aletta Winne)*, Cate---- Winne

Note that baptismal records do not exist for Schenectady before 1691, and do not exist for Albany before 1684.

Andries Hanse Barheit and his wife Geertie Teunise

Pearson states that Andries Hanse Barheit , "yeoman of ye Great Flatt near Coxhacky [sic]" had a lot next to Pieter Bronck's farm. Pearson erroneously makes the statement that "perhaps" Andries Hanse Barheit is the same man as Andries Hanse de Sweedt who lived at Kinderhook. Andries Hanse de Sweedt at Kinderhook was not Andries Hansen Barheit and descendants must be careful to distinguish between the men named Andries Hanse.

Pearson further tells us that Andries Hanse Barheit's wife was Geertie or Gerritje Teunis the daughter of Teunis Teunise de Metselaer and that she was deceased by 1699 when Egbert Teunise became the guardian of her four children.

Baptismal records for the Albany Reformed Church show many baptisms for men named Andries Hanse. Sorting them out is difficult so I will list them below with notations as to which Andries Hanse they belong to.

- 1685. Feb. 8. Johannes, of Andries Hansz. Wit.: Johannes Bekker. By Annetje Teunisz, Anna Bekker.
- 1685. July 29. Jochum, of Andries Hansen [57]. Wit.: Lambert Van Valkenborgh. By Anna Sachariasz. [HUYCK]
- 1688. March 11. Cornelis, of Andries Hansz Huyg. Wit.: Lambert Van Valkenborg. By Judik Verwey. [HUYCK]
- 1689. Oct. 13. Geertruy, of Andries Hansz. Wit.: Lucas Jansz. By Grietje Folkersz.
- 1693. Oct. 15. Barent, of Andries Hansz and Grietje Gysbertsz. Wit.: Wouter Quakelbosch, Johanna Pietersz.
- 1693. Andries, of Andries Huyk and Catryn Valkenborg. Wit.: Wilhem Peer, Lysbet Sikkels. [HUYCK]
- 1696. Nov. 11. Marretje, of Andries Hansz and Catrina Lambertsz. Wit.: Cornelis Scherluyn, Lysbeth Wendell. [HUYCK]
- 1700. Jan. 7. Margrietje, of Andries Hansen Huyk and Cathryn Lammertsen. Wit.: Robbert Levingston, Jr., Margrietje Levingston. [HUYCK]

The following list showing the baptisms of Andries Hanse Barheit's children by his wife Geertie Teunise will illustrate the naming patterns followed, and the relationships of the baptismal sponsors to the parents

Date of Baptism; Child's Name; Baptismal Sponsors
- 8 Feb. 1685; Johannes ; Presented by Annetje Teunisz. Johannes & Anna Bekker
- 13 Oct. 1689;Geertruy; Presented by Grietje Folkersz. Lucas Jansz *(possibly Lucas van Sasberge who married Maria Evertse Van Wesel)*

- 15 Oct. 1693; Barent *(possibly named in honour of Andries' mother Barentje Straetsman, Barent being the male form of the female name Barentje)*; Wouter Quakelbosch, Johnna Pietersz *(possibly Johanna Hans Barheit married to Pieter Willemse Van Slyke, using her husband-o-nymic of Pietersz/Pieterse)*

Abbreviations Used in Source Notes

DA: Deacons' Accounts 1652-1674. First Reformed Church of Beverwyck/Albany, New York. Janny Venema. 1998.

DHB: Doopregister der Hollanders in Brazilie 1633-1654. C. J. Wasch. 1889

ERAR: Early Records of the City and County of Albany and Rensselaerswyck

CARS: Minutes of the Court of Albany, Rensselaerswyck and Schenectady. A. J. F. van Laer.

CFOB: Minutes of the Court of Fort Orange and Beverwyck, 1657-1660. A. J. F. van Laer.

NNC: New Netherland Connections

RDCA: Records of the Reformed Dutch Church of Albany, New York, 1683–1809

RNA: The Records of New Amsterdam from 1653 to 1674 Anno Domini. Berthold Fernow.

Source Notes

[1] Marco Ramerini. The Dutch in Brazil: The WIC and a new Holland in South America. http://www.geocities.com/Athens/Styx/6497/brazil.html

[2] RNA. Vol. I Minutes of the Court of Burgomasters and Schepens 1653-1655 p 240. http://olivetreegenealogy.com/ships/st-charles1654.shtml

[3] GFSA p 15

[4] GFSA p 124

[5] Albany County Deeds. 6:162-163. "...and Barentje Straetsman widow and relict of the said Jacob Janse Gardenier deceased, having five children procreated by her hubsand Hans Coenraets..."

[6] NNC. V. 5 No. 3. 2000 p 78. 16 August 1659. Not. H. Schaef, 1359/106. Barentje Straetsmans, housewife of Hans Coenraets from Beerhey, now a free baker near Fort Orange in New Netherland....

[7] CFOB. p 140.

[8] A translation of the suit of Asser Levy against Hans Coenradtsen is in Samuel Oppenheim's "The Early History of Jews in New York" p 90

[9] C.J. Wasch, Doopregister der Hollanders in Brazilie 1633-1654, (1889)

[10] Descendants of Teuntje Straetsman may wish to read my book "Teuntie Straetsman and her Four Husbands: Jan Meyering, Jueriaen Haf, Tieleman Jacobsz vander Meyen & Gabriel Corbesy"

[11] ERAR v3. P 245 12 September 1663. Hans Coenraetsz, baker, dwelling in the village of Beverwyck in New Netherland. States he bought from Hans vern der Lip, late trumpeteer to Johan Maurits, governor of Brazil, half of a house on a lot granted by Maurits in Brazil at the marketplacke in Mouristat. The contract of sale was dated 27 March 1643, but now that Brazil is owned by the Portuguese, Hans wants his money for the house.

[12] Dutch women sometimes used their husband's first names in place of a patronymic, thus the term husband-o-nymic

[13] The Doopregisters of Brazil begin in 1633 but a thorough search of these records failed to turn up any more children baptised to Hans and Barentje other than the two daughters previously mentioned. We know they were in Brazil before this year (circa 1647) and the lack of a baptismal record is puzzling. However one section of the Doopregister has a brief list of names and reads *"Kinderen die gedoopt sijn, waervan de briefkens, die dieswegen in de kercke aengegeven, sonder datum van jaer oft dagh bevonden, welcke vermits die in ordre van den tijt niet conden ingeschreven worden hier per memorie genoteert en wort gegist dat deselve in de jaren 1647, 48 off 49 gepassert sijn"* (Translation courtesy of E.J.Richards <richards@uni-wuppertal.de>: *"Children which were baptised, the record of which was reported for this reason to the church, without year or date, which could not be inscribed in order, are noted by memory and were given that the sametook place in the years 1647, 48 or 49")* It is possible that the 12 year old child travelling with mother Barentje Straetsman was missed in the baptisms made from memory. It is equally possible that Barentje and Hans baptised the child in Mauritsstad, for which no records exist.

[14] CFOB V1.1920 p.242 Hans was called as a witness in a case about stolen sugar cookies

[15] They Came From Recife: the First Jews to Settle in America 1654. Dr. Kenneth Libo Ph.D and Michael Skakun

[16] http://olivetreegenealogy.com/ships/nnship77.shtml

[17] RNA. Vii p 427. 27 August 1658. Pieter Jansen pltf vs Teuntje Straaatmans [sic] deft. Pltf

delivers in court certain written complaint for the insults and abuse given him, pltf, by the deft. Deft. Admits having done so, but did not threaten him with a knife, and says the pltf abused her sister for a whore and her as one who steals. Plft denies it and says she, the deft., abused his wife as a thief, and threatened him with a knife, which Leuntje Pieters knows. Deft says the pltf abused her three times in the first instance. Parties charged by the Court to keep themselves quiet and peaceable and whichever of the two should begin again, shall pay 25 gl as a fine to the Schout

[18] NNC. V. 5 No. 3. 2000 p 78. 16 August 1659. Not. H. Schaef, 1359/106. Barentje Straetsmans, housewife of Hans Coenraets from Beerhey, now a free baker near Fort Orange in New Netherland, being a sister of Theuntke [sic] Straetsmans (the wife of Thielman Jacobsz from Caerick who sailed in 1646 on the ship Rhee van Zeeland to Brazil and who died later in Gaudeloupe, now declares in the name of her sister Theuntje Straetsmans now living in Manhattan, that she has received a full account of the wages earned by her late husband. (Note that in fact Thielman had not died in Gaudaloupe and reappeared some years later after Theuntje had remarried as his widow)

[19] ERAR V.1 p 27. 18 April 1657. Refers to himself as "Hans Coenradtsen, late soldier in the service of said company" Made his mark with a stylized dark "**H**"

[20] ERAR V3 p. 34. 24 August 1660. Power of attorney from Hans Coenraetsen to his wife Barentje Straetsman. Hans Coenraetsz, late cadet in the service of the honorable West India Company here in New Netherland, declared that by these presents he consistutes and appoints Barentge Straetskerke [sic] his wife, his special attorney to obtain..... a settlement of accounts of the wayges and pay due to him for his services..... Makes the mark "**H**"

[21] ERAR v3. P 245 12 September 1663. Hans Coenraetsz, baker, dwelling in the village of Beverwyck in New Netherland. States he bought from Hans vern der Lip, late trumpeteer to Johan Maurits, governor of Brazil, half of a house on a lot granted by Maurits in Brazil at the marketplacke in Mouristat. The contract of sale was dated 27 March 1643, but now that Brazil is owned by the Portuguese, Hans wants his money for the house.

[22] CFOB V. II p. 224

[23] CFOB V. II p. 254

[24] similar in appearance to a lemon but part of the Passion Fruit family

[25] a type of squash

[26] FDRCB p. 51

[27] ARS. V.1. p 109-110 Thursday, 14 October 1669

[28] a mudde is 3.056 bushels

[29] DA. P 234 March 30 to Hans de backer's wife, a mudde of grain

[30] DA. P 237. 26 Aug. 1672 given to Hans de backer's wife f25. 10 November 1673. Given to Hans de backer's wife 2 guilders and half for a haunch of venison. 15 November 1673 given to Hans de backer's wife in order to buy salt for half a schepel, f 4. 24 November 1673, given to the wife in sewant in order to buy soap, f6. p 253. 16 January 1673 f40 given to Hans de backer for a ship's blanket

[31] DA p 237 29 September 1672. Given to Hans de backer's wife two schepels of wheat. P 246. Given to the wife [of Hans de backer] 2 schepels of wheat from Klaes de Brabander [Claes Jansen van Bockhoven]. P 253. 10 January 1674. To Hans de backer's wife 2 schepels of wheat

[32] DA p 241. 19 February 1673. Bought for Hans de backer's wife 4 pounds of English soap at 16 stivers a pound. p 243 13 May 1673. Paid Ryckje for 4 lbs of soap which was given to Hans de backer's wife. p 245 6 August 1673. given to Hans de backer's wife 4 lbs of soap. 8 January 1674. Bought for Hans de backer's wife 4 pounds of soap

[33] DA p 241. 19 February 1673. bought for Hans de backer's wife a shirt for Hans, from Barent de smit for f10. p 245. 6 August 1673. Given to Hans de backer's wife a shirt from Aert Jacobsz' estate. P246. 26 August 1673. Given to Hans de backer a pair of pants from Jacob Aertsz' estate, which was inherited for the poor [cost] f10. DA p 249. 1 December 1673. Given to Hans de

backer's wife an Osnabruck linen bolster and a pair of pants. 27 December 1673. Given to Hans de backer 2 ells and half a quarter of dosijn

[34] DA p 250. 27 December 1673. To Barent de schoenmaker for 2 pairs of children's shoes for Hans de backer's children, and a pair of women's shoes, [paid] f26

[35] DA p 242. 26 March 1673. Given to Hans de backer's wife 4 pounds of butter from Barent de muelenaer [at a cost of] f4. P 253. 12 January 1674. To Hans de backer's wife one pound of butter

[36] DA p 253. 15 January 1674. To Hans de backer's wife one pound of sugar

[37] DA p 253. 17 January 1674. For Hans de backer one ancker of good beer, costs f 7.10

[38] DA p 243. April 1673. Given to Hans de backer's wife for half a schepel of salt and for one pitcher of wine f4.10. Also an old ship's blanket and bear skin, and two pillows from an old hemtrock and some junk from Jacob Aertsz' goods, which is estate of the poor. Also paid Jan Gou to build an oven for Hans de backer and [for] some bricks he has added to it [total cost] f20. Also to Hans de backer's wife one schepel of wheat from Swarte marten. Also 2 posts to put the oven on

[39] DA p 253. 15 January 1674. To Hans de backer's wife one pound of candles

[40] DA p 247. 20 October 1673. Given to Hans de backer's wife a haunch of venison of 13 pounds at 5 stivers a pound, bought from Johans Wendel [total cost] f3.5. 29 October 1673 given to Hans de backer's wife a haunch of venison, costs f3. DA 24 November 1673. Given to the wife [Hans de backer's] half a deer, costs f7. P 249 27 December 1673. Given to Pouwelijn and Hans de backer half a deer

[41] DA, p. 253. 18 Jan 1674. [gave] a sheet for a pall to the wife of Hans de backer, deceased.. Costs one beaver, paid for the beaver in seawant

[42] DA p 253. 31 January 1674. Given to Hans de backer's widow 4 schepels of wheat [cost] f16

[43] ERAR V2 p 18

[44] Albany County Deeds 1630-1894 6:162, 163

[45] Holland Society of New York, Marriage Record Albany Reformed Church 1683-1804, Pieter Willemsz, y.m. living here; Johanna Hansz, y.d. living here.

[46] Ship De Trouw. June 1660. The wife of Hans Coenraet, baker at Fort Orange, and 2 children 7 and 12 years old [NWI]

[47] ERAR Vol. 3 p. 415. Indenture of service of Johanna Hans, daughter of the late Hans Coenraetsen to Richard Pretty and his wife. 30 September 1674. Indenture names "Barentie Straetsman, late wife of Hans Coenraetsz, baker, deceased and now married to Jacob Janse Gardenier" and "..her daughter named Johanna Hans ... the said daughter is now over eight years old..." and binds Johanna to Richard and Elisabeth Pretty for eight years.

[48] According to "Encyclopedie van Voornamen",compiled by A. Huizinga [Amsterdam: A.J.G. Strengholt, 1957] pages 46,48, "Barentje" is the feminine form of "Barent". "Baertje" is the feminine diminutive of "Beart" of "Baart" and "Baart" is a form of "Barent". While it is therefore possible that the child Barentje was named after Pieter's mother Baertie, there are two facts that make it more likely this was not the case. Baertie's other children all named daughters Baertie (not Barentje) in her honour. Two of Johanna Hanse Barheits' siblings named daughters Barentje (not Baertje) and I suggest they did so in honour of their mother Barentje Straetsman. [Reference courtesy of Dorothy Koenig]

[49] VOSBURGH BIOGRAPHY, NY (Original pamplet can be found in New York State Historical Library, Albany, New York). Date of original pamplet 1913; Dingham Versteeg & Royden W. Vosburgh; 90 West St. New York, NY., pp. 113-130

[50] read "Teunis"

[51] read "Eal"

[52] New York City Wills, 1730-1744 Page 451.

[53] RDCA No mother named. Margriet. Sp. The father, Wouter Aartsz

[54] RDCA No mother named. Wouter. Sp. Douwe Jelisz, Aaltje Evertsz (she married first Gerrit Lubberts and second Joannes Oothout. She may have been a sister to Rebecca Evertse)

[55] GFSA

[56] C.J. Wasch, Doopregister der Hollanders in Brazilie 1633-1654, (1889)

[57] This is Andries Hanse Huyck of Kinderhook who married Cathaline/Cateryn Lambertse Van Valkenburg.

www.ingramcontent.com/pod-product-compliance
Lightning Source LLC
Chambersburg PA
CBHW060802270326
41926CB00002B/69

9 781987 938067